THE MIDNIGHT THOUGHTS

PART 2

RUDRAKSH MISHRA

Made with ♥ on the Notion Press Platform
www.notionpress.com

Contents

Contents

Preface

The Mid-night Thoughts series, is a collection of beautiful poems and thrilling short stories. Variety in genres, from social problems to love, from motivational lines to classic divine. Simple poems yet deep. Two authors, two different styles of writing combined to give reader the best of them. Hope you would like these masterpieces.

Acknowledgements

SARTHAK SINGH

Sarthak Singh, author of Mid-Night Thoughts (part 1).
He was born On 28th July 2007 In Gonda. He was Fond Of writing at a very young. He mainly write poem's and short stories. He shared his poem with some of his friend.

Social:

Instagram: @author_sarthak

RUDRAKSH MISHRA

Rudraksh Mishra was born on 6th December 2007 in Lucknow. His habit of being eager to know why and how of everything, exploring the concept of things made him unique in the crowd. He showed up interest in writing from the age of 5-6. Started his writing career with short stories and essays, sent to local newspapers got published, received a little fame in local presses. He never suppressed himself, he kept pushing himself and at the age of 13 he published his first book, it was a short article about parallel worlds.

A young author Writing from a very young age, mainly a fiction writer, writes poems relating to modern day Society. Got featured in columns of various newspapers. An internally published author. Author of The lost friend and The secret existence (only the preview is released till date)

Social:
instagram: author_rudraksh

ACKNOWLEDGEMENTS

ACKNOWLEDGEMENTS

Prologue

Contents

1. Trout of Land

I don't need anyone
In my life there's no need of fun
I just don't want enmity
I don't wanna have publicity
I thought they might be graceful
But they turned out to be powerful
Their power must be controlled
This stress, i can't hold
I think they are mad
There influence are bad
Their mind is a mess
They have cross the limits of selfishness
They wanna stop a river stream
Without thinking about its dream
They wanna slay us all
But we should bind to forestall
They wanna snuff us out
They are nothing but a trout
Their intentions are suspicious
Buy they are too capricious

2. Horrifying Night

At the mid night

It was a full moon night

No one was with me

Not even the street lights

I was left all alone

There was a Sound of walking on stone

The animals blared

I was little bit scared

Suddenly, a shadow was there

There's something unfair

There was slight noice

I think it was shadow's voice

I sneaked behind the tree

I asked if there's anyone

I started feeling stress free

Because there was no reply, there was none

3. Fear Recurred

Of being, linked
The thought recurred
He was once again, allured
But it was all ruptured
It was all going good
Didn't know where he failed
Was smiling very often
Don't know what he faced
Wanna give one more chance
Wanna change the reality
Still having a regretful stance
Don't wanna accept the reality
Was it a dream
Or a nightmare
Don't wanna lose her
Living with a fear
Living with a broken heart
Still fixing all the cracks?
Got addicted to be alone
Now, wanna live along cracks

4. Line of Truth

People feel bad
By knowing the truth
People become sad
Just not to face the truth
They don't care
About what people think
They don't care about the feelings
They do whatever they want
They are losing interest
Just showing fake care
Wanna be someone's interest
I Got played once,
Now more aware
Still lost in old thoughts
Those pretty days
That i bought
Those dreamy nights
That i heard about
Wanna live those days again
Wanna feel those nights again
I, Don't need anyone
To share my pain

Just want another chance
And just wanna think again
Not about them
Only about my pain

5. Oceanic Drown

it feels like i m drowning in a ocean of thoughts
it feels i m lone travelling in a season of drought
feels like am just a toy
a toy they use for their joy
a toy through they wanna ploy
it's all about killing my joy
I wanna be alone
but i can't
they wanna ruin me
but they can't
my mind is drowned,
as if i am crowned
the king of depression
Forgot how to make decisions
i found myself lost
lost in deep thoughts
no one cares for me
no one cares for my thoughts
i wanna have someone
who supports in good times
i wanna have someone
who doesn't leave in bad times

these are only my thoughts
drowning in an ocean
and so like my thoughts
I'm drowning in depression

6. Fake World

In my life
There's dark everywhere
The night has arrived
It seems There's dark worldwide
No one believes me
No one cares for me
In this fake world
I think, No one needs me
I got ignored
And was left all alone
My thoughts remained unexpressed
My smile was even there, as if a clone
From everyone whom, I expected
will say a hii!
I got only disrespected
While talking to me they feel shy.
They paved the way,
For my depression.
They paved the way,
For my execution.
I think it's the time to end the game
Eyes blinking, heart pumping, life too lame

I don't want any fame
I just wanna end this game
The better I explained
The better they denied
And Now,
Everyone saying the last bye

7. Immaculate heart

I am confused
Not for the future
Don't know how to live in present
Forget about the future
Confused whom to trust
Also, lost everyone's trust
Confused, how to express
I think, I am depressed
people say I'm immature
but i need some serious care
could stay a lil longer here
i just need some serious cure
It's not my fault
I know, I do overthink
But my heart,
Doesn't let my eye blink
Don't wanna see a dream
Which is gonna be broken
Don't wanna see a dream
Which is nothing but, taken

8. Forbidden Poet

I was very potential
but fell mentally ill
was feeling very joyful
having deep pain still.
People got changed
i got caged
mind got raged
still surprised why i changed.
Spell they cast
ideas not too vast
decide too fast
their decision is the last.
I have some flaws
flaws that are trickier
i am just so inferior
as i am no superior.
People made me infeior
they don't wanna me to grow up
they wanna me to remain inferior
of their thought, I am fed up.
Don't know what to do
confused with my life

people don't care about it
they're just playin with my life.

9. The Lost Soul

I Think I Have Been Lost
I Am Priceless, I Have No Cost
It's A Rain Of Frost
I Think, I Am Dead Almost
I Wanna Go Afar
I Wanna Be Infinite, Like Star
They Wanna Me To Rend
But Of Them, I Am Not Offend
I Wanna Say It Clear
But They Don't Want To Hear
They Are Not Like They Appear
But Of Any, I Have No Fear
They Have Lost Their Hope
Because The Habit Of Tope
Their Activity Are Like Steed
But They Are Sowing Their Enemy in Their Own Seed
They Don't Wanna To Hark
They Love To Live In Dark
There Passion Is To Slay
With Other's Life They Wanna Play

10. Pain in Rain

Yesterday i saw a swain
he was all alone in heavy rain
i think he was in pain
he was not having words to explain.
He has done many travail
but i think he was fail
the night was stygian
for him it was a bad luck rain.
He was lost in his own thought....
for his mistake he has been caught
i think he was having some fear
that's why he doesn't want to hear.
I think he is depressed
i also know he is suppressed
i think he wants to confess
but he also has a burden of stress.
He stood at rain to behold
his story is still untold
it was a shivering night of cold
when he wanted to fight, but he got scold.

11. My mind speaks

My life is a lie
everyone saying the last bye
Them not caring for my feelings is worst,
realising it late is really worst.
My Mind Is Still Developing
But It Knows Everything
It's The State Of Beginning
Also The State Of Wondering
I wish i could know if it was a coincidence,
Or it was showing sequence of consequences
The habit of talking everyday turned into,
the habit of ignoring and stalking everyday
I think it's the time to end the game
eyes blinking heart pumping, life too lame
Who cares ?, infact
who stays?
Faced many loses
never expressed to anyone
silence does not discloses
now, don't wanna trust anyone

12. Till Infini

You will be my life
for my entire life
no one can replace you
It's my promise to you.
The feelings I felt
I think It's now sealed
my emotions are theft
now, there's no feeling left.

You have my heart
you paved ur way through my heart
your reside in my heart
none, only u r in my heart.
I'll love you till
the end of infinity
you are mine still
and will remain my priority.
I get lost in your eyes
eyes get wet in your byes
i still have our memories
those are better than my luxuries.

13. One Day Yoga

Remembered yoga day once again
Just doing a formality
They do care
Pretending once again
Here just for clicking pictures
Instead of doing yoga
Just interested in giving poses
Not even interested in yoga
It's good for mental health
But just for once in a year?
Trying to be mentally fit
But just for once in a year?
Can't live without pretentiousness
They aren't mentally fit
I'm the eyewitness
Just pretending Being socially fit
There's no need of showiness
Don't try to be pretence
Try to live in reality
Society won't accept your showiness
I just wanna say
Don't be patriot for just one day

Have a great and Happy Yoga Day

14. Habitual of You

I was lost in myself
Broken or obsessed with myself?
I've lost every hope
Hope to again live for myself
Now, I realised my life without you
It seems like there's no reason
For me to live without you
Still, Habitual of living with you
I tried to move on, but
Confused what I'm thinking about.
Still finding a peace in you,
Still, Habitual of living with you
Wanna loose all those memories,
But, Still wanna live those memories
Again, that I've spent with you
Still, Habitual of living with you

I think, It was worse for you
Is that the reason,
That you never tried to talk to me.
Is that the reason,
That you never had a trust on me

I hope to live again for myself,
Maybe I can just say this.
But you know it better,
Because till now you did this.
I know you moved on,
But, have you ever thought about me.
Ever thought about my love,
I'll forget what you did to me
I just need you as my love
I really tried to move on, but
Still, Habitual of living with you

15. Being a poet

Being a citizen, i hold few right
isn't that true
Being a critic, i told few views,
never been viewed, isn't that you
Being a poet, I write my heart
you think they too harsh
Being an artist, I present my heart
you think they too trash
Being a liar, you do praise me
wait do you wanna hail me
Being a driver, you do wanna steer me
wait you can't control fired wings
Being a boy with vision, can't stuck in illusions
Being a boy with goal, can't fall in hole
Being a boy with dreams, can't get lost in dreams
Being a boy with passion, am not lost in old fashion

16. Troll and Roll

maybe i am not social
maybe i am not any special
maybe i am not that spiritual
maybe i ain't in any co-circular
may i got a small circle
but i got a brother to burgle
maybe i don't go to b'day parties
but i do success parties
maybe i leave and rest
but i do observe the best
maybe i express less
but i don't careless
maybe i am not doing for a while
but going through hell, isn't a lie
maybe i am not the best
but still better from the rest
maybe i am not good in looks
but have my name on books
maybe i am not famous in school
but world famous, isn't it cool.

17. Wandering in my mind

Living my life, not sure what is right
fighting with my mind, i am not doing it right
controlling my anger
discussing with so many langers
Empty mind, devil's house
People with no mind, devil's spouse
I was the one who was left
Without any treasures i was theft
Living in a magical world
believing in a world of tragic heards
Stop giving me motivating words
I dont wanna live in a world of stupid heads
They pretend to be wild
but they behave Like a child
they show care for me
are they really concerned for me?
They wanna achieve their goal
they have dirty mind as coal
they pretend to be cool
or they just wanna make us fool.

18. Cursed Angel

To the valley of demons,
where i may find any of my ancestors
can someone contact their command centers
the place is beyond all the hells.
They must be waiting for me to die
so that i could be able to go back
they tellin my brain to say the last bye
they are sending message to jump off and never look back.
The day i went back up there
i realised things are different up here,
I have my own palace there
unlike fellas like phallus here.

Besides the luxuries
here a couple of beings love me
this is where i belong
people i could get along.
Was wandering in a wrong planet
planet of sick minds
a place full of secret homicides
died in a planet draping their heids.

People are not hateful or racial
resting in my palace i got to know
i am the naughty fatal angel
no doubt i m the cursed angel.

19. Midnight Thoughts

Woke up in the middle of the night
done seeing no brighter light
done seeing no win over fight
were they really right?
Wondering am i alright mentally
they fought coincidently
they burgled quite accidentally
were they really right?
Moon was guiding in the darkness
problems were breaking into the address
from birth painting the gloominess
were they really right?
Done fighting with the rival
am done hoping for survival
trusties misleading to fossorial
were they really right?
Embodied in december
still have flashbacks to remember
dawn is surely there in voice of amber
were they really right?

20. My Friend

The day was black
Time was all that i lack
The way had a crack
still my friend held my back
I lay on my couch
had meds ready in my pouch
was being a slouchy
still my friend held my back
Thought of going on a walk
had none to accompany my walk
saw worms slothing on my walk
still my friend held my back
Switching the channels
realised i was being dismantle
broke as lost every contention
still my friend held my back

21. Ruining my Mind

Want to go far from this fake world
for my sake, wanna go away
Way too much is running in my mind
thought scrabbling in my mind
that ruining my mind
please don't mind.
I spit facts
facts that hurts
hurts, i got wound and scars
scars in my mind
mind, please don't mind.
Hoping for a good day
day no way no good
livelihood is so plastic
drastic, aren't they dramatic
Classic, is that replica jurassic
sick, sick mentally and physically
physically they lay, mentally they play.

22. Friendship like dove

Under the bright light
wonder was the place right
eyes glanced, heart jumping and
pumping, so good wish the moment freezed
shouldn't be that shy
eyes were amazed, how to suppress
wish could say the last bye
heart was confused, how to express
I swear i gave my best
but believe me i got the worst
The better I tried
The better I failed.
How Wonderful bond that was
can't tell how grateful i was
the friendship was like dove
not sure when it turned love

23. Gloomy

I was furious one day
was damn curious that day
Life seemed hilarious that day
Everyone was suspicious that day
That day was all black
my problems were all back
wish I could pack them in a sack
wish I could send them back
In past there was a boy
He was full of joy,
but was used like a toy
wish could have joy like the boy.
One day, he was standing all alone
that day, he realized he fought all alone.
He was in pain and was crying
everything was in vain, rain covering his tears.
He realized what happiness is
he found it's just mere piece of crappiness.
So childish to search for happiness
in this dark world of selfishness.
Happiness is not what we get,
the conditions aren't always met

is this a permanent fault
or it's just a mental hault.

24. Occasionally Good

Every year environment day is celebrated together
have been
Ten people taking selfies by planting a tree
Slogans are also being written and posters are being made.
Calling children, getting them to write essays
How many trees are cut to make the paper
decorating the green leaves on the same paper
Everyone is gathering enthusiastically from far and wide
Coming in AC car to do environment program
Speeches are also going on, on the environment
It's very hot, so in the hall the AC is on
Cold drinks are running in the arrangement of water
And the eco freaks are eating in plastic

25. Inner Thoughts

I thought it was a day to rejoice
but, it was a worry in disguise.
I thought it was a juncture to enjoy
but, it was a picture to annoy.
I thought it's time for a come back
but, good time is all i lack.
I thought it's all majesty
but, incidents were all nasty.
I thought it was a new bright ray
but, it was just a single good day.
I thought god is against my favor
but, it's just the people too clever.
I thought it was a bad timming
but, it was executed with planning.
I thought it was a peice too rare
but, it was sold for free in the fair.

26. Surprised How

Races are limited
colours are limited
people are limited
surprised how faces are infinite in the world.
Gifts are limited
products are limited
swifts are limited
surprised how rifts are infinite in the world.
Needs are limited
diet is limited
living cost is limited
surprised how greed is infinite in the world.
Supplies are limited
fulfillment are limited
deeds are limited
surprised how lies are infinite in the world.

27. How Close They Were

Something wrong with me
No one really bothers me
I know
I'm not perfect
But, I also know
That I'm trying to be myself
Maybe i am wrong
Or maybe my parents are wrong
Maybe I'll be happy,
By what I'll do
Maybe they thought about
What should i really do
Facing many challenges
Still searching hope to live
Silence doesn't discloses
Still searching reason to live
I know my potential
But, I fell mentally ill
Pretended to be very joyful
Having deep pain still

Look how close they were,
Look how folks they were.
Look how loving they were,
Look how erratic they were.
I'm really trying hard
I just need their regards
Ours they said, hours they spend,
flowers are dead, friendship came to end.

28. Childhood Days

I'm losing everything
my edges are being killed
stealing my interest for everything
my childhood is being killed.
They want me to leave
it's all they please
sometimes that's all I believe,
to die and live in peace.
I wonder if am in right place
wonder if i am a part of race
wonder if am just in a hace
wonder am i dying at low pace.
They're only killing my intentions
living in a world of pretensions
intentions those were pure without hesitation
they livin in a world busy in presentation.
They want me to mess up
pack up and leave
but i'll back up i believe
they want me to sit and give up.
I just believe in myself
still wanna remember

those giggles and laugh, still miss myself
those childhood days still wanna remember.

29. Soul Cries

The Ascent Of My Mind

That Wants Me To Look Behind

But There's No Feature Of Rewind

Having Dust In My Eye, But I Am Not Blind

I am not blind

i can see what's happening with me

the night i slept crying

i wept my tears lying

Is That A Mountain?

That They Wanna Climb

Or is it a Fountain?

That They Wanna Find

They Wanna Make Me Cry

Our Thoughts May Vary

I Am Not Afraid, There's No Worry

They Are Still Waiting For Me To Bury

My Mind Is Still Developing

But It Knows Everything

It's The State Of Beginning

Also The State Of Wondering

30. Cryptic Pen

The power of pen is dead
I lost my pen,
to the depressive bed.
I followed the way it led,
now, am alone, they all fled.
I believed it'll go till end
confused why they took,
i didn't lend.
If i ask they will send,
Shocked, it was my end.
From flyin high sky
rock bottom now i lie
carryin bag of dreams i cry
fighting demons,
by smiling i lie.
Nothing now makes sense
loving songs by sense
hidden with bruises,
by the fence.
Blood coming from eye,
need new lens.

31. Witch-Craft

Going by a tough phase
using smile to fight the haze
too many layered faces,
the reason for me to faze.
A small connection,
got even smaller.
To get over it,
I became a baller.
My mind cryin in head,
like a halker.
Have their identity hidden,
as a person in true caller.
Witch-craft that's all i am facing
with ghosts, all i am racing.
With a bag of wil,
it's all gracing.
With a crack in head,
Creativity is all i am gaining.

32. Feelings burried

The day snakes attacked
was the i was born
The day i laughed
was the day i was born.
The day lightining hit me
was the day i felt alone
The day smile hit me
was the day laugh left.
The day i heard diss
was the day i realised this
The day i try to criticise this
was the day they try to diss.
The day faces turned back
was the i decided to win
The day theh sent me out
was the day notioned to begin

33. Let me flex

I write to stay alive,
wanna say things on live.
Mind goin high like mt. Clive,
makin money like honey in a hive.
They say i am goinh down,
dish, i am not a clown.
Heavy head makin me drown,
Still flexin best in town.
Gonna rise up for my throne,
rush makin jams like bison in yellow stone.
Fightin with innerself all lone,
frusted wanna shout on a microphone.
I accept i am not good,
but i don't need plastic, thanks i am good.
Maybe a little talented, oh! touch wood,
rage eating my body, like fire and wood.